Walking Into Your Destiny!

Walking Into Your Destiny!

SAMETRIA ALEXANDER

AuthorHouse™
1663 Liberty Drive
Bloomington, IN 47403
www.authorhouse.com
Phone: 1-800-839-8640

KJV
Scripture quotations marked KJV are from the Holy Bible, King James Version (Authorized Version). First published in 1611. Quoted from the KJV Classic Reference Bible, Copyright © 1983 by The <u>Zondervan</u> Corporation.

Published by AuthorHouse 11/04/2014

ISBN: 978-1-4969-5081-9 (sc)
ISBN: 978-1-4969-5082-6 (e)

In dedication to…

I would like to dedicate this book to my husband (Dexter Alexander), who so lovingly supports all that God has called me to do. Who without his love, patience, kindness, and trust I would not have turned into the woman who I am today. To my spiritual mother and father (Apostles Lee and Davida Harris) who saw the best in me and believed in my ability to touch lives even when I doubted myself, and to my friends, my loved ones, and to all who have supported me through reading my books and passing God's message. Last, but certainly not least, to all who have a passion to walk into their destiny and use their spiritual gifts…May you walk into it and be blessed!

Introduction

Destiny! This word alone should be enough to excite you! The fact that God loves you so much that he has already mapped out for you a path in which all you have to do is walk into it should excite you! The wonderful thing about destiny is that one is never too young or too old to experience it because destiny is personal. Before you were shaped, before you were thought about by your parents, and before your eyes saw the light of day, they saw God's glory first. He called you by name and appointed you in the beginning.

It amazes me when I hear people say that they do not believe in destiny. Most people think that they are in control of their own destiny. You will notice that people who say this are individuals who want to make their own way in life because things are not happening fast enough for them. These individuals would rather take the path of least resistance.

The truth is sometimes there is some resistance when you are walking into your destiny. However, God wants you to know that the resistance that you are experiencing is only to prepare you mentally and spiritually for what you are about to walk into. If God gave us everything that he has in store for us right away with no resistance involved, why would we need faith? Why would there be a need to believe in God and to have hope? The resistance is to build our faith, our minds, our hearts, and to prepare us for greater.

You have a destiny. Yes, I am talking to you. Maybe you do not know what it is. However, you should rest assured in the fact that you have one. Sometimes it is not knowing 'when', but knowing 'who'. And the 'who' is God. He has loved you since the beginning - not your beginning, but HIS beginning, and he has mapped out a future for you. Now, it is time for you to walk into it!

Before you can walk into your destiny you must first seek he who created your destiny. If God has spoken your destiny, it will come to pass. Isaiah 55:11 states, "So shall my word be that goes out from my mouth; it shall not return to me empty, but it shall accomplish that which I purpose, and shall succeed in the thing to which I sent it." God's word says it (your destiny) SHALL come to pass. God is so great that everything that he speaks and everything that he has spoken over your life has to come to pass just because of who he is.

It is a scary feeling when you do not know why you are on this earth. I remember as a little girl I used to ask God all the time, "Who am I? I mean I know what my parents call me, but who am I?" Even at a young age I always wanted to know my purpose on earth. God wants you to know right now that part of walking into your destiny is knowing your purpose here on earth.

You may not know this, but you were made for a purpose. When God made you he had a purpose in mind that only you would be able to fulfill. As a matter of fact, Ephesians 1:11 states, "In him we have obtained an inheritance, having been **predestined** according to the **purpose** of him who works all things according to the counsel of his will." God is trying to tell you that you are not just leftover junk. It does not matter how you got here. The important thing is that you are here, and with purpose!

CHAPTER 1

Activate your Covenant

God has infinite wisdom. It is very important to understand that he has already mapped out, planned out, and executed every detail of your life. This alone should give you some kind of comfort. All you have to do is trust in him. Even when you have made your own decisions and things have gone awry, God's word still says that, "all things work out for the good of those who love God and who have been called according to his purpose" (Romans 8:28).

The last part of that scripture is very important. Yet, so many people leave it out when quoting it. So, know this: Because you LOVE God and have been CALLED by him, he is going to work everything out for you. I do not know about you, but this scripture makes me overjoyed!

Let us break this scripture down even more with these two action verbs. Because you **love** (action verb) God, and God has **called** (another action verb) you according to his purpose, you have a covenant with God that no demon in hell can break. This covenant covers you through everything that you will ever go through in life. He has already spoken this covenant since the beginning of time.

Knowing and believing this scripture are two different things. To know is one thing but to believe is a totally different thing. When you believe God's word you have made yourself the same with what GOD says. When you believe God's word you have also activated the covenant that you have with God. You have activated everything that God has in store for your life. Blessed be the name of God!

It is important for you to get this. You believing God's word about your future and your destiny only activates the things that he has in store for you. Your destiny cannot be fulfilled without you first believing that 1, God has created you with a purpose in mind, and 2, that EVERYTHING in his word is true. I believe that this is what compels God to move in our lives. So, I ask you today: Do you believe or do you just know? Are you merely existing or are you activating your covenant with God? Are you ready to walk into your destiny that God has set aside just for you?

The covenant of God will not lead you astray. However, what it will do is open doors that need to be open or close doors that need to be shut. It will shine a light on you that will have others wondering why this glory surrounds you. People will be drawn to you because they can see that glory, and they will want it too. The covenant of God will leave you and your family blessed. This covenant of God gives you the same covenant that God promised Abraham. God promised Abraham many, many descendants and nations. You, my friend, are under that covenant because you have chosen to be the same with God's word.

God is ready to take you to that next level that he has promised you. He is ready for you to walk into your destiny. From this point on God says, "There is no looking back." Your belief has just activated all things supernatural for you. The spiritual realm has opened up for you and there is nowhere to go but to the top! No more do you have to wonder what your purpose in life is. God is about to activate that purpose and your destiny. No longer do you have to feel inferior to those around you because God is about to make you superior. Your destiny is going to allow him to use you as a vessel to help those around you. Get ready to be in awe of his majesty! God says, "I have heard your cries at night. I have felt your pain and apprehension. Because you have believed in my word I can now show you my glory. No longer will I hold back any good thing from you!" Thus, says the Lord!

CHAPTER 2

The Pursuit of God

Ask yourself a question, and be as honest as you can with yourself. What are you in pursuit of? For many people its money. For many people its careers, fame, education, family, cars, and other material things. I'm here to tell you that unless one's pursuit in life is God, life will continue to go in a circle.

Have you ever watched a dog chase its tail? Not only is it funny, but it is pretty pathetic. The dog is going in circles seamlessly to do something that seems to be impossible. It is the exact same way with us. We tend to want to make our own way in life. We focus so much on what we want that we care little about what God wants for us. When one way does not work out we try another way, and another way, and so on. Then, after all the hard work and all the going back and forth, we end up right back where we started- tired and out of breath. We have figuratively chased our tails. When we begin to understand that the key to true happiness in life lies only in our relationship with God, we can truly begin to live our best lives.

It is written on more than one occasion in the Bible how to receive from God all that he has for you. If you have ever read the story of King Solomon then you know that he was one of the richest and wisest Kings who ever lived. God appeared to him in a dream and told King Solomon to ask for whatever he wanted. Now, most people who get this request from God would immediately ask for money or fame or something else materialistic. King Solomon, however, asked for pure wisdom from God.

Because he asked for wisdom, God was pleased with his answer and promised King Solomon wisdom plus riches and honor, and a long life. He also told King Solomon, "As for you, if you walk before me in integrity of heart and uprightness, as David, your father did and do all I command, and observe my decrees and laws I will establish your royal throne over Israel forever" (1st king 9:4). God was setting the tone in the beginning. Matthew 6:33 also states, "But seek first his kingdom and his righteousness, and all these things will be given to you as well."

You may be asking, "What things?" God says, "All things!" Whatever you have a want for and a need for God will supply for you if only you would humble yourself before him and seek him diligently. Your answered prayers are in God's word. Your answered prayers are in your relationship with God.

When I was 26 years old I decided I wanted to go to school and get an education. I felt like if I could only get an education that I could be someone great in life. Little did I know, I was already great in the eyes of God. So, I went to school for four years and then went another year for grad school. All the while thinking that this piece of paper I was getting was going to validate me in some way.

I wish I knew then what I know now. I have already been validated through Christ. In the beginning of time, before my parents had even thought of me, God had a one on one with me and named me a writer. He put in me everything that I would ever need to fulfill my purpose on earth. Yet, I 'chased my tail' for years. All I did in the end is dig myself into thousands of dollars of debt. I did not need an education to do what God had already ordained me to do. I am writing now. I am using the gift that God has placed in me.

Please do not get me wrong. I am in no way saying that one should not get an education. However, what I am saying is that if God has placed something in you he is going to make sure it comes out-education or not. God is bigger than anything man made. Some people need higher education to pursue medical degrees and other professional degrees, and some people will not need it. This is where your relationship with God comes in. He will show you and direct you and open all the doors that need to be opened for you.

God is great, and because God is great you are great! God needs you to understand this and to believe this. Again, I tell you, before you were even born God had a one on one with you that he did not have with anyone else. He called you and ordained you. He placed in you everything that you would ever need to fulfill his purpose and destiny for your life. It is time to stop putting things and circumstances in front of God. He is bigger than any circumstance and he will work it out for you if you only allow him to.

CHAPTER 3

Your Best Life

God did not place you here to live a mediocre life. He placed you here to live a great life. Simply put, God wants you to start living your best life now. Jesus says in John 10:10, "I come that they might have life, and that they might have it more abundantly." Even knowing this scripture many of us still wrestle with things that allow us not to have an abundant life.

We wrestle with depression, weight issues, finances, health issues, addictions, generational curses, doubt, fear, low self-esteem, and many other afflictions. This is simply because we have not made ourselves the same with the word of God. If God says that we should have an abundant life, if we really believe God's word, then that is exactly what we should have. Yet, we allow situations and different afflictions to deter us from our God-given right to have a great life.

I am not sure what the word 'abundance' means to you, but in my mind it means overflow. When there is an abundance of something there is more than enough to sustain you. When you are living an abundant life you have an abundance of good health, happiness, confidence, bravery, self-esteem, and the likes. When you are living an abundant life you wake up every morning knowing that you are walking in the promises of God.

Do you want to live in abundance? Many will say yes, but many will not change their actions to tap into this abundance. You may be asking yourself, "How can I tap into this?" It is easy. You do this by changing your way of thinking, speaking, and then changing your lifestyle. I believe that what one thinks, one is or one becomes. Even

God's word states, "Death and life are in the power of the tongue, and those who love it will eat its fruit" (Proverbs 18:21).

What fruit are you eating? Are you telling yourself daily that you are defeated? Are you looking in the mirror and calling yourself fat? Are you telling yourself that you are depressed, broke, busted, and disgusted? Then sadly, that is what you will be until you make up your mind that this is not you.

For many years I suffered from depression. I can remember at a young age being sad all the time. This depression followed me through adulthood. After I divorced my first husband, I made the decision to get placed on medication to control my moods. This medicine that I was on made everything ok. It made me immune to anything that went on around me. A few years later, I got off the pills. However, I was still suffering from depression.

After I had my last child, I went back on medication. At that time, I was a stay-at-home mom. I was home all day, so I was more into my own feelings and thoughts. I did not have an outlet to keep the spirit of depression away. I took the medication for a few months and got off again. I was determined not be depressed. People who do not suffer from depression may wonder why people become depressed. People who are depressed do not even know why. Contrary to what many doctors have said, depression is an attack from the enemy.

When one becomes depressed they are wrestling against spiritual demonic forces. Ephesians 6:12 states, "For we wrestle not against flesh and blood, but against principalities, against powers, against the rulers of the darkness of this world, against spiritual wickedness in high places." Doctors and pharmaceutical companies would like us to believe that depression is from a chemical imbalance. However, it is my belief that they want us to believe this for financial gain.

Many people may not like this statement, but I am here to tell you that God's word does not lie. Depression can be eliminated through spiritual warfare. Since our weapons of warfare are not carnal, you have to fight spiritually. Come against any depression, low self-esteem, and fear by casting them into the very pits of hell from which it originated. Bind them up in the name of Jesus. Change your way of thinking and find outlets. This is what I had to do. While it was no easy task, I have been able to defeat the enemy. I pray constantly and immerse myself in God's word. I speak life to myself.

Weight is another issue that affects many people in the world today. Every time you turn on the television there is pressure to be skinny. Also, every time you turn on the television there is pressure to eat. Eating can turn into an addiction if one is not careful. This is where most weight gain comes from-an addiction to food. Addiction to food can also be caused from depression.

Sadly, I also had an addiction to food. Food made me happy, so I ate. I did not think about portion size or what I was eating. I just wanted to eat. In 2013, my husband and I went on a cruise. I just remember being so unhappy on that cruise because I was so overweight. When I left for the cruise I was 165 pounds. For me this was too much because I was only used to weighing 130 pounds at the most. I knew

I had to do something about it that would be permanent. I had to do two things: change my lifestyle, and change my way of thinking. I decided no longer would I live to eat, but I would eat to live.

When I got back from the cruise, I made the decision to go on a weight challenge. I was going to eat right and live healthy. Immediately, I cut all the things out of my diet that I loved- sodas, sweets, red meat, and pork. I began to only eat chicken, fish, turkey, water, and healthy snacks. I did this for 24 days straight. By the time I got finished, I had developed a habit so much so that I did not want to go back to my old routine. I lost 20 pounds, and I am still maintaining it. For me to do what I did took a change, and now I am in abundant health. I walk at least three times a week to keep my body and my heart healthy, and it feels great!

I have told you this to tell you that you can live your best life too, and you can start now. This is what God wants for you. If you are not living your best life it is going to be impossible for you to walk into your destiny. It will be impossible for you to fulfill your purpose on earth. Please do not waste any more of your life feeling sorry for yourself. God has promised you an abundant life full of overflow. Will he not give it to you? Do you not want it?

Right now, in the name of Jesus, I bind any demonic force in your life. Whatever is stopping you from living a life of overflow is now cast down into the very pits of hell from where it originates. I declare and decree a fresh anointing over your life right now in the mighty name of Jesus. I declare and decree a life of overflow in all areas of your life. I call forth a new mind set in you right now. I call forth new actions in your life right now. No more will you wake up feeling defeated. Instead, may you now wake up with expectations of an abundant new life. May you walk in the promises of God and have a zeal for life that supersedes any doubt that you ever had. In Jesus name I pray. Amen!

CHAPTER 4

What Are You Scared Of?

Fear is a natural emotion that humans have. However, fear is a carnal emotion. Any time the Bible speaks of carnal it relates to one's physical, worldly, or earthly being. Serving God is a spiritual experience. This means that our carnal mindset has to be put to rest.

If you were to ask many of your friends and family members why they are not pursuing their dreams the number one response would likely be fear. People tend to fear the unknown. Usually, when we cannot see what is in front of us, fear and anxiety kicks in. However, Timothy 1:7 states, "God has not given us a spirit of fear, but of power, and love, and a sound mind."

God wants you to know that he has placed something in you that only you can bring into fruition. Because of this reason alone, you have no reason to fear. God is ready for you to let go of your fear and step out of your comfort zone. You may be feeling uncomfortable right now because you are walking into your destiny. God wants you to know that this uncomfortable place is what is going to get you to fulfill your true destiny in life.

As Christians, we must learn to get uncomfortable when it comes to the things of God. Being uncomfortable brings forth our faith in God and his plan for our lives. Being uncomfortable in the things of God also allows us to receive from God all that he has for us. Simon, in the Bible (Luke 5:4), was a fisherman. After toiling all day and catching no fish, God asked Simon to go into the deep and let down his net for a catch.

Simon, in the beginning, did not want to do it. He was uncomfortable. However, he submitted to God's will and cast out his net. At that moment, Simon came out of his comfort zone. He was tired from fishing all day, and then God told him to go into deep water. However, doing so allowed Simon to catch so many fish that his net could not even hold them!

This is what God wants to do for you. He wants to give you so much that you will not have room to contain it-once you become a fisher of men. Yes, God's destiny for you is going to allow you to touch the lives of others. It is going to allow you to plant seeds in people that would not otherwise be planted without meeting you, and to increase your life as well. Are you hearing the voice of God telling you to do something? Well do it! God will never steer you wrong. If he tells you to do it, he is going to make sure that you are already equipped for it. Fear plays no part in this.

I can remember all my life having a relationship with God. I can also remember while in middle school God telling me that I was going to speak to many people. To be honest with you, it scared me. Years went by, and 17 years later what he spoke over me came true. Was I scared? Of course! The very first time I had to do it I literally wanted the floor to open up and swallow me whole! However, God had already equipped me with what I would need. All I had to do was let go of fear.

Fear will trap you. It is a trick of the enemy that will halt any and all plans that God has for you. Fear will have you thinking that you are not good enough. Fear will have you questioning God. Fear will leave you stagnant in this purposeful life that you are supposed to be living.

Today, God wants you to guard your hearts and minds from the power of fear. It is time for you to launch yourself into unfamiliar territory. Part of getting rid of fear is trusting in the one who made you. His will is perfect for your life and can only come into existence if the power of fear does not exist.

Fear and purpose do not mix. It is like water and oil. No matter how hard you try, you will never live your appointed life in fear. Know this: every hair on our head is numbered.

It is up to you what you will do with it. It is possible for one to have quantity of life with no quality. That is exactly what fear does- allows one to live with no quality of life. Today, speak quality over your life.

CHAPTER 5

Don't Lose Sight

Out of all the five senses that humans have, it is my belief that the most vital one is our ability to see. I say this because what one sees can determine where one is headed. When you are walking into your destiny it is of high importance that you do not allow what you see to halt your faith in God's plan for your life. God wants you to know that what you see is not where you are going to end up.

What a person sees has the ability to shift that person's faith. Hebrews Ch. 11:1 states, "Faith is the substance of things hoped for and the evidence of things not seen." If we were to break this scripture down, it simply means that even though we cannot see a thing, we believe that it will still happen. This is faith: believing what you cannot see.

When we lose sight of where God is taking us we hold up not only God's progress, but our own. You may be believing God for something Right now, but your current situation appears as though you will never get there. Keep believing! God may have spoken a word to you years ago and it still has not come to pass. Keep believing! When you have faith in God and are trusting him entirely, he has no other option but to take care of you.

Right now, you may feel stagnant because God has you immobile where you cannot move front, back, left, or right. Doors seem to constantly close in your face. Have you ever wondered why? It is likely because this is where he wants you in order to renew your faith. But, please understand that if he has you in a place he will take care of you. God has not brought you to a place to leave you. In his word he never promised us that we would not endure hardships, but one thing he did promise is that he would never leave us nor forsake us (Deuteronomy 31:6).

When one allows sight to shift his or her faith, that person's faith has not only shifted, but the atmosphere has shifted too. God cannot work in an atmosphere where faith does not exist. Even his word states, "Without faith it is impossible to please God" (Heb. 11:6). Now is the time to shift the atmosphere to a conducive state where God can work. This may require you to put away your carnal eyes and put on your spiritual eyes. This may require you to grab hold to what God has promised you since the beginning and run with it. God has already spoken, now he needs for you to believe. Once the atmosphere changes God's glory can then come upon your life. His work will begin to flourish in you both spiritually and physically. Once the atmosphere changes the enemy has to flee and turn lose everything that has been held from you for so long.

I see you walking into your destiny! When you get there a change is going to come about you that not even you can explain. Your walk will be lighter, your spirit will be higher, and your sense of sight will be keener. Before, you were only seeing what existed, now you are able to see what does not exist but what can and will exist through your faith in God. Do not lose sight of where you are going. For where you are now is not where you are going to end up!

Chapter 6

Press on!

I often say that life is not a pain, but it is a strain. An important thing to remember about life is that challenges come only to make us stronger. So, during those challenging times we must push through and strain through until we reach the place that God has for us. When a person strains it is usually difficult. Imagine yourself walking up a very steep hill with your very life depending on whether or not you make it up that hill. Well, I am sure if your life depended on you walking up that hill that you would indeed put your all into it and make it to the top. You would push yourself and strain yourself until you finally made it.

This is what God wants us to do as it relates to where we are going in life. He wants us to push past adversity. Push past rejection. Push past hurt. Push past generational curses. Push past divorce. Push past death. Push past depression. Push past guilt. Push past what is behind you. Push past what is in front of you. Push, knowing that the pushing of your spiritual being heightens your physical.

It was Paul who stated in Phillipians 3:13, "But one thing I do: forgetting what is behind me and straining towards what is ahead. I press on towards the goal to win the prize for which God has called me heavenward in Christ Jesus." Even Paul understood that he had to push to get to his destiny. Paul could have let his past deter him. However, Paul was able to rise up and strain towards the mark that God had set for him. Because of Paul's determination to push through his adversaries, Paul became a well-known Apostle for Jesus Christ to the church spreading the gospel and touching lives tremendously.

God wants this for you as well. He has a mark for you to get to but it is going to take some pushing and some straining. God wants you to know that you are almost there! You may feel tired and out of breath, but your mark has almost been reached. A little further and you will be there! All this straining that you have done and are doing is equipping you for your destiny. Do not question God as to why things always seem harder for you and everyone else gets of easy. God is saying right now, "You are special and I have created you to do a work that only you can do. If I let everything come to you easy, it will not build your faith. I am building your faith!"

God is trying to build your faith in him through this strain of life. However, strain does not necessarily have to yield pain. The strain of life will yield perseverance, faith, confidence, leadership, and strength. These are things that God needs for you to have to run this race called life and to move into your destiny. Now is the time to put your arms out and one foot in front of the other. Move forward with strength and strain to the finish line!

CHAPTER 7

Light your fire!

You may be wondering what fire I am talking about. I have come to tell you that there is a fire that burns inside of you that has been burning since your beginning. Right now it may be a small flame, but soon it will be a raging fire. God wants you to ignite this fire and let it blaze!

The fire that I speak of is your spiritual gift. Yes, you have one. Everyone who breathes has one. As a matter of fact, some have more than one. Does everyone use it? No. But I am willing to believe since you have taken the time to read this book that you desire to put your spiritual gift to use. In 2nd Tim 1:6 Paul states, "Fan into flame the gift of God, which is in you through the laying on of my hands." The gift of God is already in you. In the beginning of this book I explained to you that before you were even formed God had a one on one meeting with you. He has already anointed you, appointed you, and sanctified you for whatever gifts he has given you. All you have to do is use them.

There are many in the body of Christ and many gifts. The body of Christ needs your gift to stay aflame, and your flame cannot burn if you never use your gift. This so important for you to grasp. Ask yourself a question: What is the use of fire if it cannot stay lit? There is no use. So, what's the use of you having a gift if you are not going to use it?

God has touched my heart to help everyone whom I come in contact with to realize their purpose and destiny on earth. There are so many people that want to know what their gift is but have no idea. I must be honest with you: I cannot tell you what your gift is, but if you have tapped into the Holy Spirit he has already showed you.

If I were to use myself as an example, it is no surprise to me that my gift is writing. My very first day of kindergarten was me anticipating learning to read. Throughout my childhood years I would write stories and poetry. I always wanted to become an author. However, what I never had the idea of doing is speaking, but it is another one of my gifts. God has appointed, anointed and sanctified me as a writer and a speaker. A person without this gift may not be able to understand how I can take a blank sheet of paper and fill it with words. But it works the same way. I am not able to understand someone else's gift, nor is it meant for me to.

When we start worrying about the gift that God places in others we have taken the focus off what God is trying to build in us. You must ask God to speak to your heart. If you are still and listen you will be able to tap into your gift. Often times, we already know our gifts but we have fixed our minds to make us think that something is not our gift. Now is the time to change your mind of who you think you are. Now is the time to tap into what you are. What you are is a child of the King who loves you so much that he gave you gift/s to use for his glory. He took one look at your spirit and saw fit that you have all the talents and gifts that you have today.

God made you special, unlike no other. Your fingerprints are even different from anyone else's in this world. Therefore, your gift is your gift. Yes, there may be others with the same gift as you, but no one can perform that gift like you. Your gift is your gift that God has given all to you. Your personality is going to make it unique. No one else will ever be able to touch it. This knowledge should build your confidence. God does not want you to look left or right. However, he wants you to look to him and stir up the gifts that he has given you.

There is no better time than today to begin operating in your anointing. Declare to yourself today that you are anointed above all that God has placed in you, and start operating in your gift. For too long you have been walking around aimlessly and questioning your existence in life. The enemy would have you to believe that you have no purpose, but know this: Everything that God made was made for a reason, and you are no exception to this rule. You were made for a reason. Now is your season to begin reaping all that God has placed in you. Fear plays no part in this time of your life. God wants you to walk forward in faith knowing that he is with you always.

CHAPTER 8

Persevere with Confidence

Everything that you have read so far is to help you. Think it not strange that this book is in your hand and that you are reading it. I am the appointed vessel that God wants to use to reach you. I am not saying that this book will land into the hands of the masses. However, what I am saying is that God is speaking through me to touch the lives of those whom he has appointed to read this book. I write this in confidence knowing that my obedience to the will of God will allow me to touch exactly who needs to be touched by this book at the appointed time.

God wants you to move forward in the same confidence. You may not be the next world famous person as you begin to use your gifts, but you will be well-known to the people whose lives whom you touch. You will impact them in such a way that you will forever be etched into their minds and hearts. To you, what you are doing is small, but when you begin to see the impact of all the lives who you are going to touch it turns into a big thing to God.

God desires that you persevere in your gifts. The only way you are going to do this is through faith in the God who gave you these gifts, and a confidence in yourself that you can do it well. Hebrews 10:35 states, "So do not throw away your confidence; it will be richly rewarded. You need to persevere so that when you have done the will of God, you will receive what he has promised." The confidence in your gift is what is going to allow you to persevere.

God wants you to know today that it is okay to be confident in your gifts (as long as that confidence does not turn into cockiness). It is okay to have confidence because everything that God is telling you to do he has already equipped you with. This confidence that radiates from you will allow you to be anointed in your gifts, and these gifts will begin to flow easily from you. The faith you place in God in your ability to deliver your gifts will allow you to persevere even when others around you are being judgmental.

The last part of that scripture says that when you have done the will of God you will receive what he has promised you. What has God promised you? Whatever it is I want you to know that you are getting closer and closer to these promises being fulfilled. It is impossible for you to do God's work without him doing your work. This is scripture, "That if you delight yourself in the Lord he will give you the desires of your heart" (psalms 37:4). Is it not a delight to use your gifts for the benefit of the kingdom? Then delight in it! Psalms also tells us that when we commit our ways unto the Lord he shall bring it (promises) to pass (Psalms 37:5).

It has been a long time coming for you. God wants you to know that he has not forgotten about you. The voice of

God is saying: "The time is now." My prayer for you is that God evokes in you a 'right now' spirit. The gift is already in you, and now is the time for you to begin walking in the confidence that you were already born equipped. Therefore, you are already ready. The time for you to persevere is now!

CHAPTER 9

You are Already Anointed!

As it pertains to your anointing, it is so important for you to know that God has placed your anointing on you. Because of this fact, your gift is not something that you have to go and get from God. Your gift is something that has already been placed inside of you. God is not saying to you, "I have something for you, come and get it." However, he is saying, "I have placed something in you, start using it!"

There is no better time than now to start operating in your anointing. It has already been there since the beginning of time. The Bible tells us in 1st John 2:27, "But the anointing that you received from him abides in you, and you have no need that anyone should teach you."

No one can teach you what God has already placed in you by his spirit. Because his spirit is upon you, you are equipped to do what you may feel to be the most difficult of tasks. The spirit of the living God, when placed upon you, gives you power. This is the same power that abided in Jesus's disciples to heal the sick and cast out spirits. This same power has been placed inside of you. This power then recoils from you and transcends upon the masses. Once this happens, you become powerful in your gift.

There is a difference between someone who has a talent and someone who has a gift and activates that gift through the spirit of Jesus Christ. A talent does not always touch others, but a gift that is activated through the spirit will outshine any talent. Now is the time for you to activate God's spirit within you. Think about it: if it was not intended to be used, it would not have been placed inside of you!

I want you to remember this: you belong to a great God and because of this, you are great! For so long you have been setting dates as to when you are going to begin using your gift. These dates have come and gone and you still do nothing. God has sent me to tell you that today is the day. God wants you to move forward in confidence. Trust the one who created you, and let God's spirit work through you. He will never lead you wrong!

CHAPTER 10

The Prayers of the Righteous....

You may be contemplating at this point where you go from here. It is actually quite easy. From here you pray. The bible not only tells us to pray without ceasing (1st Thes. 5:17). But it also tells us, "Call to me and I will answer you, and will tell you great and hidden things that you have not known" (Jeremiah 33:3). God has some hidden things he has been keeping from you-until now. He is now ready to truly reveal his glory to you like never before because you are ready to truly give yourself to him.

He is waiting for you to simply pray and ask him to uncover those hidden things that are so great for your life. He knows that these hidden secrets that are just for you are going to move you to the next phase of your life. Through your prayer life, your gifts and talents will be revealed to you. His word plainly states, "Ask, and it shall be given to you; seek, and you shall find; knock, and it shall be opened up to you" (Luke 11:9).

Now is the time to get out of the mind frame that God is withholding something from you. His word states, "For Jehovah God is a sun and a shield: Jehovah will give grace and glory; No good thing will he withhold from them that walk uprightly" (Psalms 84:11). All you have to do is pray, ask, believe, and you will receive. Your gifts may be hidden from you and even man, but through your prayer life, what God has placed in you since the beginning of time will reveal itself.

Right now, I speak revelation over your life. Through this revelation, your gifts will begin to easily flow from you through the spirit of the living God. Through your prayer life God will begin to show you your future. Your future is brighter than what you think it is!

I cannot express to you how important it is to maintain your communication with God. He is your power source that is going to activate your gifts and allow you to walk into your true destiny. Communication with God is also your power source that keeps you connected to using your gift/s. I urge you right now to talk to God in the morning! Talk to God in the noon day! Talk to God in the evening! Talk to him even in the midnight hour. You will find that it is in the midnight hour that he will begin revealing his plans for your life. I decree right now that God is going to reveal so many incredible things in your life! You will wonder why he sees you so worthy to do these things. It is because he has called you since the beginning of time! My prayer for you is the receiving of direction, revelation, and even confirmation of the things to come for you. In Jesus name walk in faith and expectations of your destiny!!!!!!!!!! Amen!!!!!!!!

Prayers

Prayer for gifts and talents

Dear Heavenly Father,

I come to you as humbly as I know how. As your son/ daughter it is my desire to know what my gift/s is that you have placed within me. Your word tells me that you have known me even since the beginning of time. You had a one on one with me and anointed me appropriately with my gift through your spirit. Today, I call forward the gifts that are in me that I may use them to touch the lives of others. I ask that you place in me a 'right now' spirit to begin using my gifts. No longer do I want to keep pushing back the time on when I will start. Father God, today I choose to walk in my anointing. I believe that no one can use my gifts the way that I can. You have equipped my spirit, my mind, and my body to be used to glorify you. No longer will fear and trepidation play any part in my life. Today, I move forward in confidence knowing that the one who has anointed me and appointed me is the one who reigns forever. Thank you God for loving me so much that you gave me such wonderful gifts, and even when I am unsure of my gifts may you allow the Holy Spirit to place a burning in my belly for clarification. In Jesus's name I pray.

Amen!

Prayer for boldness

Dear Heavenly Father,

I come to you today asking for a holy boldness to come upon me. Allow this holy boldness to penetrate my very being, and move me forth in confidence knowing that it is your spirit that evokes a flame. This flame was placed inside of me through the laying on of hands, which occurred between you and me even before the beginning of time. Father God, help me to realize that you have not given me a spirit of fear, but of power, love, and self-control. This power that comes from you gives me the ability to touch lives and enter places by the blood of Jesus. Today, I ask that you evoke in me a bold spirit. Anoint my feet and hands. Wherever my feet tread and whatsoever my hands touch may it be blessed. In Jesus's name.

Amen!

Printed in the United States
By Bookmasters